2|21

OPIOID EDUCATION

TREATMENTS

FOR OPIOID ADDICTION

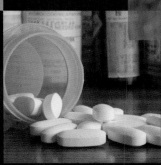

OPIOID EDUCATION

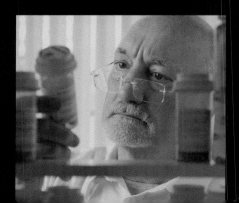

OPIOID EDUCATION

TREATMENTS
FOR OPIOID ADDICTION

AMY STERLING CASIL

MASON CREST
PHILADELPHIA | MIAMI

MASON CREST
450 Parkway Drive, Suite D, Broomall, Pennsylvania 19008
(866) MCP-BOOK (toll-free) • www.masoncrest.com

Printed and bound in the United States of America.

CPSIA Compliance Information: Batch #OE2019.
For further information, contact Mason Crest at 1-866-MCP-Book.

First printing

ISBN (hardback) 978-1-4222-4385-5
ISBN (series) 978-1-4222-4378-7
ISBN (ebook) 978-1-4222-7432-3

Library of Congress Cataloging-in-Publication Data on file at the Library of Congress

Interior and cover design: Torque Advertising + Design
Interior layout: Tara Raymo, CreativelyTara
Production: Michelle Luke

Publisher's Note: Websites listed in this book were active at the time of publication. The publisher is not responsible for websites that have changed their address or discontinued operation since the date of publication. The publisher reviews and updates the websites each time the book is reprinted.

QR CODES AND LINKS TO THIRD-PARTY CONTENT

You may gain access to certain third-party content ("Third-Party Sites") by scanning and using the QR Codes that appear in this publication (the "QR Codes"). We do not operate or control in any respect any information, products, or services on such Third-Party Sites linked to by us via the QR Codes included in this publication, and we assume no responsibility for any materials you may access using the QR Codes. Your use of the QR Codes may be subject to terms, limitations, or restrictions set forth in the applicable terms of use or otherwise established by the owners of the Third-Party Sites. Our linking to such Third-Party Sites via the QR Codes does not imply an endorsement or sponsorship of such Third-Party Sites or the information, products, or services offered on or through the Third-Party Sites, nor does it imply an endorsement or sponsorship of this publication by the owners of such Third-Party Sites.

CONTENTS

KEY ICONS TO LOOK FOR:

Words to Understand: These words with their easy-to-understand definitions will increase the reader's understanding of the text while building vocabulary skills.

Sidebars: This boxed material within the main text allows readers to build knowledge, gain insights, explore possibilities, and broaden their perspectives by weaving together additional information to provide realistic and holistic perspectives.

Educational videos: Readers can view videos by scanning our QR codes, providing them with additional educational content to supplement the text. Examples include news coverage, moments in history, speeches, iconic sports moments, and much more!

Text-Dependent Questions: These questions send the reader back to the text for more careful attention to the evidence presented there.

Research Projects: Readers are pointed toward areas of further inquiry connected to each chapter. Suggestions are provided for projects that encourage deeper research and analysis.

Series Glossary of Key Terms: This back-of-the-book glossary contains terminology used throughout this series. Words found here increase the reader's ability to read and comprehend higher-level books and articles in this field.

Anyone can become addicted to opioids—even well-educated medical professionals who understand the dangers of these drugs.

 WORDS TO UNDERSTAND

chronic—an illness that persists for a long time.

euphoria—a feeling or state of intense excitement and happiness.

illicit—forbidden by law; illegal.

prescription—an instruction written by a medical professional authorizing a patient to receive a medication.

CHAPTER 1

WHO NEEDS TREATMENT FOR OPIOID ADDICTION?

While serving as a doctor in the US Navy, "Alison" helped to treat an American president and a high-ranking senator, among thousands of other patients. When she left the Navy and began working at a hospital in Appalachia, Alison was regarded as one of the best, most reliable doctors. She dispensed drugs to patients safely for over eighteen years, but never considered using them herself. Until one day her husband, a nurse who misused fentanyl, introduced her to powerful opioids.

Within six months, Alison was injecting sufentanil several times a night. She hid syringes in her clothing and injected secretly everywhere in her house, in her car, and after working out at the gym. Sufentanil is the strongest opioid available—five to seven times stronger than fentanyl, and a staggering 4,500 times stronger than morphine.

Alison appeared happy to outsiders. On the inside, her marriage was falling apart, and her addiction was destroying her life. "During that time, that was the only thing I looked forward to. That was really the only thing that was good in a day of life for me," she said.

In 2016, nurses at Alison's hospital began to suspect that she was stealing drugs from the hospital and using them. Alison was caught and immediately lost her job. To keep her medical license, Alison had to complete a ninety-day residential treatment program designed for medical professionals. Then, she would have to complete a five-year follow-up program that included regular meetings with other recovering healthcare professionals along with drug monitoring.

More than 70,000 Americans died of drug overdoses in 2018. Most of these deaths involved opioids.

Alison hopes to regain control over her life, but she's still in the process of recovery. She's part of a Physician Health Program (PHP) that's offered by the majority of US states. PHPs provide some of the best drug treatment available. The kind of long-term treatment that Alison benefited from is too expensive or unavailable to most people who are addicted to opioids.

About 100 people a day die from opioids, according to STAT, the health website affiliated with the *Boston Globe*. Opioid overdoses are the leading cause of death for Americans under age fifty. STAT surveyed health policy experts at ten leading universities, who predicted that the opioid epidemic will get worse before it improves, and that it could lead to the deaths of up to 500,000 Americans over the next ten years. The kind of treatment Alison received is needed by millions of Americans, but it may be too expensive to provide.

Who Is Most At-Risk of Opioid Addiction?

Most people are aware of the dangers of street drugs like heroin. **Prescription** opioids and street heroin are all very similar drugs with different ways that they are manufactured and taken. These drugs are called "opioids" because they all produce similar effects as the original opioid, the juice of the opium poppy.

According to the Centers for Disease Control, taking prescription opioids for longer periods of time or higher doses increases the risk of addiction, also called opioid use disorder. Prescription opioid use is also a risk factor for the use of street drugs like heroin, which can also be mixed with extremely strong, dangerous opioids like fentanyl. The National Institute on Drug Abuse (NIDA) reported that 75 percent of people who received treatment for heroin addiction in the 2000s started out using prescription opioids. Among heroin users in large cities, 86 percent started out using prescription painkillers, NIDA's studies learned. Anyone who takes opioids is at risk of developing addiction.

The current opioid epidemic began in the late 1990s, when family doctors started prescribing opioids for **chronic** pain. Before the 1990s, strong painkillers were only prescribed for severe pain and end-of-life conditions like terminal cancer. Or, they were used primarily in hospitals, where their use could be carefully supervised, and not prescribed for patients to use at home. The increase in painkiller prescriptions corresponded with increased emergency room visits, addiction rates, and deaths resulting from overdoses.

Teens are at high risk of prescription painkiller and opioid abuse. According to the NIDA, prescription drugs are the fourth most commonly abused substance (after alcohol, marijuana, and tobacco) among young people between the ages of twelve and seventeen. Teens most often get prescription painkillers from family or friends, but some are prescribed painkillers after sports injuries. The National Institute of Drug Abuse's annual Monitoring the Future survey reported in 2018 that 60 percent of teens who misused prescription drugs bought or received them as a gift from friends or family.

Older adults between the ages of fifty-seven to eighty-five are also at-risk of prescription opioid addiction. Many older adults receive prescription medication for pain. More than half of this age group uses more than five medications or supplements a day. Drug interactions and frail health contribute to the risk of addiction.

Veterans, chronic pain patients, and "opioid naïve" patients are also at higher risk of addiction to opioids, including prescription pills and illegal drugs.

Studies indicate that older adults are at a higher risk of becoming addicted to prescription painkillers.

What is Opioid Dependence and Tolerance?

You will hear the words "dependency," "tolerance," and "addiction" when people talk about opioids. Opioid dependency and addiction are not the same. Everyone who takes opioids for longer than a few days will become dependent on them, but not everyone who is dependent on opioids will become addicted. Dependence means that the body has adjusted to the drug and the person needs to take the drug order to feel "normal." People who use opioids for a long period of time also develop tolerance. Tolerance means that they require more and more of the drug to feel pain relief or in the case of **illicit** opioids, experience a "high" feeling. When people who've taken opioids for a long time stop taking them, they will suffer physical withdrawal symptoms.

Dependence and tolerance aren't related to a person's "willpower" in any way. Opioids change the way that the body's central and peripheral nervous systems work, and this causes the drug dependency. This is why opioid drugs relieve pain, but also cause side effects, including constipation, dry mouth, and serious symptoms like body tremors.

"Brain abnormalities resulting from chronic use of heroin, oxycodone, and other morphine-derived drugs are underlying causes of opioid dependence," according to doctors Thomas Kosten and Tony George, who wrote an overview of how opioid dependence results from physical changes that the drugs make in the body and brain.

An opioid drug user who tries to stop taking the drug will experience unpleasant and powerful withdrawal symptoms, including strong cramps and muscle tremors, headaches and dizziness, difficulty breathing, sweating or skin-tingling sensations, and nausea or diarrhea. These occur because the body has become dependent on the drug in order to function properly.

ROCK BOTTOM

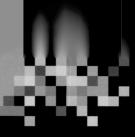

Melissa Cohen is a twenty-nine-year-old Vermont native whose addiction to prescription painkillers led to abuse of street drugs, including heroin. Melissa's addiction hit its lowest level when she found herself sleeping in a local park. After completing short-term and long-term rehab programs funded by the state of Vermont, Melissa is in full recovery and working as a barista at a healthy living store.

Over time, the body and brain of a person who takes opioids adjusts to the drugs, functioning normally when they are taking the drugs, but malfunctioning when the drugs aren't present. The symptoms that occur after a person stops taking opioids are called withdrawal symptoms. They can range from agitation, sweating, nausea and vomiting to tremors, seizures, severe depression and anxiety, and abnormal heart rhythms. Dr. Kosten and Dr. George found that the physical changes that cause dependency usually went away after a period of detoxification (detox).

A person can be dependent on a drug but not addicted. Before someone who is addicted to opioids can begin to recover, they have to give their body the opportunity to heal from dependency and move beyond withdrawal symptoms. Detox is usually conducted under medical supervision and may include treatment with drugs that improve withdrawal symptoms and help people be more comfortable during the difficult withdrawal period.

How People Become Addicted

The way the opioids work contributes to addiction. The longer someone uses opioids, the greater the chance they will become addicted. Up to 20 percent of people who use prescription opioids longer than three months could become addicted. Over 80 percent of people who are addicted to and use illegal street heroin started out using prescription opioids.

Opioids work by attaching to opioid receptors. These are specialized proteins on neurons located in the brain and other parts of the nervous system. Once they are in our bodies, opioids mimic our body's own natural pain-relieving neurochemicals, which is how they relieve pain. They also cause the brain to release chemicals like dopamine and serotonin, which cause a burst of **euphoria**—feelings of happiness and well-being. This burst of pleasurable feelings is what users call a "high."

Scan here for a short video showing how opioids change the brain:

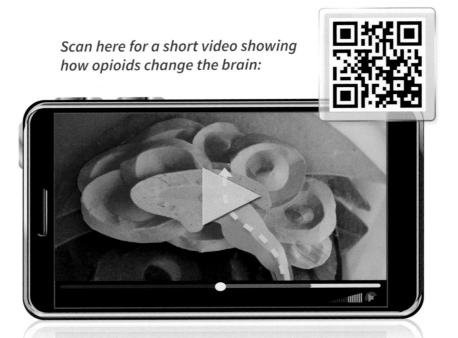

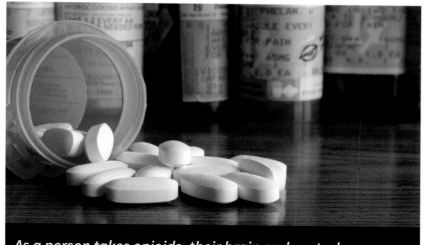

As a person takes opioids, their brain and central nervous system changes.

When they enter the body, opioids change the body and nervous system. When they bind to opioid receptors, both prescription and illicit (illegal) opioids flood our bodies and minds with positive neurochemicals like dopamine. After opioids wear off, users tend to feel more depressed and anxious than they did before they took the medication. They also tend to feel more pain than they did before. At the same time, the body craves more of the drugs, believing it will feel better. According to the National Institute on Drug Abuse (NIDA), "Nearly all addicted individuals believe at the outset that they can stop using drugs on their own, and most try to stop without treatment."

All of these changes that opioids cause in the brain and nervous system contribute to potential for addiction and are the basis of the brain theory of addiction. The brain theory of addiction is the basis for today's treatments for addiction, from behavioral therapy to medications that can help people to recover.

Some medical professionals mocked the brain theory of addiction when it was first proposed. In the past, people thought that drug addiction was a moral failing, or that it resulted from a lack of willpower. With a better understanding of how drugs affect the brain, this theory of addiction has become accepted science in addiction recovery and treatment.

Opioids cause a cycle of reward and pleasure that is controlled by the opioid, not the person who is taking the drugs.

Long-term opioid use reduces the brain's ability to respond to a natural "feel good" chemical that it releases, dopamine. Less ability to respond to dopamine directly causes depression, anxiety, and reduced mental functioning. The longer a person takes opioids, whether legal or illegal, the greater chance they have of developing addiction. Many people aren't aware that everyone who takes opioids for longer than a few days will develop physical dependence, and it's likely they're not aware that between 8 and 12 percent of people who take opioids will develop opioid use disorder (OUD), the medical term for opioid addiction.

The Symptoms of Addiction

People are diagnosed with opioid use disorder (OUD)—or addiction—when they show signs and symptoms that their use of opioids is harming their health. Behavioral symptoms include using opioids more often than they are prescribed or intended to be used and taking them in increasing amounts. When people attempt to use less of the drug or stop taking it completely, but can't take less or stop, they have another warning sign of addiction.

Life impact is one of the most important ways addiction is diagnosed. If someone who is taking opioids spends most of his time using them, trying to get more of them, or recovering from taking them because he feels sick, then it's likely he's addicted. People who are addicted to opioids may abandon work and family responsibilities. They can completely lose interest in healthy activities they used to enjoy.

Psychological symptoms often include anxiety, depression, low motivation, and irritability and anger.

Over time, extensive use of opioids, whether they are prescribed or illegal drugs like heroin, will include undesirable physical side effects and severe health risks, including overdose. Opioids always cause constipation due to their effect on nerves in the digestive system. They can also cause nausea, reduced appetite, difficulty sleeping, confusion, and

Depression and anxiety are among the symptoms of someone who has become addicted to drugs.

heart and breathing problems. Opioids slow the heart and breathing. They are a central nervous system depressant. An opioid overdose turns fatal because the drugs slow the user's heart too much and breathing comes to a stop.

Unlike an infectious disease that can be cured, drug addiction is a lifelong, chronic disease that can be treated and improved, but not cured. Addiction can be managed, and people who are addicted can stop using drugs and enter recovery. A person who is in recovery is not using drugs and can resume the activities of a normal, non-addicted life.

Who Is Addicted to Illegal Opioids?

According to the Centers for Disease Control, there are about 600,000 heroin users in the US, and most of them are under age thirty. Prescription pills, real and counterfeit, are sold on the streets, along with illegal opioids like heroin. Ultra-strong opioids like fentanyl, carfentanyl, and other synthetic opioids that come from China and Mexico are sometimes mixed with heroin or pressed into pills. About 80 percent of people who use street opioids started out taking prescription drugs. Young people ages twelve to seventeen start out taking prescription drugs they find at home or get from friends. The drugs are so strong and addictive they can turn to street drugs because of the cycle of tolerance and addiction.

"I began using OxyContin at age sixteen; it didn't take long before I was addicted," said twenty-two-year-old Amanda, a resident of Denver. After getting hooked on the drug, Amanda began using heroin because it was cheaper than the prescription painkiller OxyContin. Amanda went between the streets, home, and hospitals using heroin until she finally stopped blaming herself. With her family's help, she began a lasting recovery from heroin use.

Women and Opioid Addiction

Men are more likely than women to abuse any type of drug, but research has begun to show that when women use opioids, they are at a greater risk of addiction. According to Dr. Kirtly Parker Jones at the University of Utah, women are more often diagnosed with pain and anxiety than men, and tend to become addicted more quickly than men. Dr. Parker found that about 4.5 million women in the United States abuse some type of drug. Long-term studies conducted by

Geisinger Health System in Pennsylvania analyzed the records of more than 1.2 million patients, revealing that the "average" prescription painkiller patient treated for an overdose was a fifty-two-year-old woman.

Women are more vulnerable to addiction to opioids because they tend to have a higher percentage of body fat and lower percentage of body water than men. As a result, their bodies react differently to drugs that are fat-soluble, including opioids like OxyContin and other time-release prescription drugs. Compared to men, women have higher rates of depression, anxiety, and post-traumatic stress.

According to the National Institute on Drug Abuse, "Women often use drugs differently, respond to drugs differently, and can have unique obstacles to effective treatment." Research conducted by the Centers for Disease Control and other organizations indicates that women can be more susceptible to cravings for drugs and more vulnerable to relapse. Relapse and cravings are phases in the addiction cycle that can halt recovery and lead to increased risk of overdose or other serious health problems.

1. How do opioids cause dependency and tolerance?
2. What is Opioid Use Disorder?
3. How many women in the United States abuse some sort of drug?

RESEARCH PROJECT

Consult reliable internet sources to find individual stories of addiction and how people helped themselves and recovered. Read the stories of at least three people who were addicted to opioids and who have entered recovery. Write a one-page essay that discusses the differences and similarities you learned from the personal stories. In your essay, be sure to write about what the people who were addicted and in recovery did that helped them to stop using opioids and recover. Document your sources at the end of the essay.

Since ancient times, the whitish sap of the opium poppy (papaver somniferum) has been collected and dried to create a pain-relieving drug.

 WORDS TO UNDERSTAND

elixir—a medicinal or magical potion.

pernicious—having a harmful effect, especially in a gradual or subtle way.

sedative—a substance that promotes calm and induces sleep.

tincture— a concentrated herbal extract made by dissolving the plant in alcohol.

CHAPTER 2

OPIOID DRUGS AND ADDICTION

The history of opioid pain relievers and non-opioid analgesics dates back thousands of years. Throughout history, humans have been seeking ways to relieve pain. For example, some indigenous people of North America used to chew the bark of the willow tree to relieve pain. Scientists later discovered that willow tree bark is rich in salicylic acid, the primary pain-relieving compound in aspirin.

There is evidence that opium poppies were used as painkillers in one of the earliest human civilizations, around 3,400 BCE in the region known as Mesopotamia (present-day Iraq and Syria). The ancient Sumerians who lived in Mesopotamia called opium poppies *hul gil*, meaning "joy plant." During the centuries that followed, ancient Greeks, Persians, and Egyptians also cultivated opium poppies for their pain relieving, sleep-causing juice. Opium was introduced to China and India through traders traveling the Silk Road during the sixth and seventh centuries.

In the 1700s, the British Empire conquered India and gained control of large opium poppy fields. British traders began selling the drug in China, where millions of people became addicted to opium. The Chinese emperor tried to outlaw opium and stop the British trade. Conflicts known as the Opium Wars were fought from 1839–42 and 1856–60, but the Chinese efforts to end the opium trade ultimately failed.

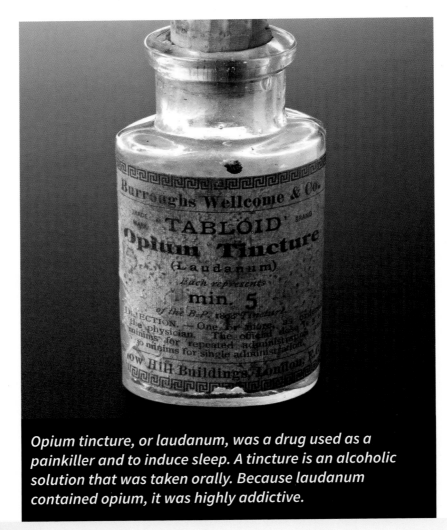

Opium tincture, or laudanum, was a drug used as a painkiller and to induce sleep. A tincture is an alcoholic solution that was taken orally. Because laudanum contained opium, it was highly addictive.

Doctors began concentrating opium juice in laudanum in the sixteenth century. Friedrich Serturner discovered morphine in the early nineteenth century. German pharmaceutical company Bayer synthesized two very different painkillers at the end of the nineteenth century: aspirin and heroin.

Throughout the twentieth century, chemists synthesized the narcotics that are used as prescription painkillers today, from hydrocodone and oxycodone to fentanyl, which is 100 times more powerful than morphine. In the twenty-first century, opioids more powerful than fentanyl continue to be created, including sufentanil, a drug that is ten times stronger than fentanyl.

Opium in the Ancient World

The ancient Sumerians and Assyrians, cultures that lived 4,000 to 5,000 years ago in the Middle East, prepared opium to relieve pain and hasten sleep by scraping poppy capsules with iron scoops and storing the juice in clay pots. The modern word "opium" comes from the ancient Greek word *opion*, meaning "poppy juice."

The ancient gods the Greeks associated with opium indicate how they used the drug: Hypnos, god of sleep, and Morpheus, god of dreams. Many years later, in 1805, the German chemist Friedrich Sertürner distilled a powerful painkiller from opium. He called the drug "morphine," a name derived from the Greek god Morpheus, because of its **sedative** effects.

Homer, the Greek storyteller of *The Iliad* and *The Odyssey*, wrote about opium's ability to relieve pain and induce sleep in both of these epic poems. Roman armies used opium to relieve pain from battle injuries and notorious Roman emperor Nero used opium overdoses to poison enemies.

During the tenth century, Persian culture was at its height as part of the Islamic Golden Age. The great Persian scientist Avicenna is credited with many innovations in medicine. Avicenna wrote a treatise on opium and its medical uses, but he also reportedly almost died from an overdose of the drug.

Painkiller of the Middle Ages

During the fifteenth century, a Swiss chemist and doctor named Paracelsus developed a painkiller that he called laudanum. It was a **tincture** of opium in alcohol. In the sixteenth century, a British doctor named Thomas Sydenham refined Paracelsus's recipe, making laudanum into a potent medication that was easy to bottle and sell.

The popularity of laudanum led to an opium epidemic in Europe and North America during the seventeenth and eighteenth centuries. The drug's influence can be seen through the popular literature of the period. British writer Thomas DeQuincey wrote *Confessions of an English Opium Eater* about his addiction to laudanum. In Bram Stoker's gothic novel *Dracula*, the vampire Count Dracula puts his victim Lucy's maids to sleep by giving them laudanum. The British poet Samuel Taylor Coleridge was inspired to write his famous poem "Kubla Khan" after waking from a dream he had experienced while under the influence of laudanum.

During the 1800s, laudanum was available in Europe, the United States, and Canada in grocery stores, restaurants, and even at candy stores. It was less expensive than alcohol, and became a universal treatment for many ailments. People used the drug to soothe crying babies and treat health problems from coughs to headaches.

The addictive properties of laudanum gradually became known. Samuel Taylor Coleridge wrote extensively to his friends about his laudanum addiction. In addition to affecting his physical health, Coleridge recognized that at times he would say or do anything to get the drug. In 1814, he wrote to his friend John Morgan, "I have in this one dirty business of Laudanum an hundred times deceived, tricked, nay, actually & consciously LIED."

Wars over Opium

The nineteenth century Opium Wars between Britain and China began with another type of addictive drug introduced to China by Western traders: tobacco. In the fifteenth century, European sailors brought tobacco to China to trade for Chinese silk, china, and carved jade and furniture. China already had opium and the Chinese mixed the two drugs together. So many Chinese people became addicted to tobacco and opium that Emperor Zhu Youjian outlawed its

The British Navy attacks Chinese port defenses during the First Opium War, 1840. The conflict forced China to open its ports to British merchants, some of whom wanted to sell opium produced in British India.

use in 1644, but by this time, it was too late. By the end of the seventeenth century, about 25 percent of the Chinese population smoked opium mixed with tobacco.

The most addicted Chinese people smoked pure opium in pipes in "opium dens." In the early nineteenth century, the British East India company gained control of opium fields in India. Their monopoly on opium would be more valuable if they could sell the drug to China's large population, but because the Chinese emperor was concerned about drug addiction among his people, the government destroyed British opium shipments and outlawed its sale.

In order to keep the opium trade going, the British attacked China and fought naval battles between 1839 and 1842 in the first Opium War. One aspects of the treaty ending the First Opium War resulted in British control over the Chinese port of Hong Kong. Other Chinese cities including Canton, Shanghai, and Macau, were also permanently opened to trade with the West.

Chinese addicts smoke opium in an "opium den" in Manila, the Philippines, during the 1920s.

Opium still was not legal in China after the first Opium War. In 1856, a Second Opium War was fought to force China to make the opium trade legal. By 1860 this war was over, and China was forced to accept opium imports legally. Opium use was so common among the Chinese that Chinese immigrants who came to the US to build railroads and work in gold mines during California's 1949 Gold Rush brought opium with them and established "opium dens" in many western US cities.

Morphine in the Civil War

Morphine is ten times stronger than the opium from which it is derived. During the American Civil War, which lasted from 1861 to 1865, doctors regularly used morphine to relieve injured soldiers of extreme pain. Morphine was called a "wonder drug," but an estimated 400,000 Civil War veterans became addicted to it. Family members of soldiers who had been killed or injured also turned to morphine or laudanum to relieve their grief and pain.

To learn about the gruesome nature of Civil War medicine, scan here:

In 1868, Horace B. Day wrote *The Opium Habit*. In this book he detailed the emerging understanding among medical professionals that although morphine and opium relieved pain, use of these drugs also resulted in devastating addiction. Day wrote that the war created thousands of addicts, including, "Maimed and shattered survivors from a hundred battle-fields, diseased and disabled soldiers released from hostile prisons, anguished and hopeless wives and mothers, made so by the slaughter of those who were dearest to them, have found, many of them, temporary relief from their sufferings in opium."

Opium Misuse Leads to Early Laws

During the early part of the twentieth century, President Theodore Roosevelt became so concerned about opium misuse and addiction that he appointed Dr. Hamilton Wright to be Opium Commissioner for the nation. In 1911, Wright told *The New York Times*, "Of all the nations of the world, the United States consumes most habit-forming drugs per capita. Opium, the most **pernicious** drug known to humanity, is surrounded, in this country, with far fewer safeguards than any other nation in Europe fences it with. China now guards it with much greater care than we do; Japan preserves her people from it far more intelligently than we do ours, who can buy it, in almost any form, in every tenth one of our drug stores."

By 1914, Congress passed the Harrison Narcotics Tax Act. The law restricted sale and use of opiates and cocaine and was the first law of its type ever passed in the United States. Morphine and opium remained available for medical use, but heroin became illegal to make, import, or sell in 1924 when Congress passed the Anti-Heroin act.

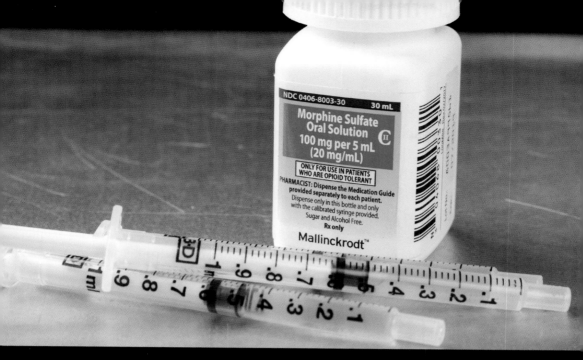

Morphine is a potent painkiller that is still used to treat chronic pain. Due to its addictive properties it is often only dispensed in a hospital setting or under the direction of hospice nurses.

Heroin for Mothers and Children

Heroin was first discovered by a British chemist in 1874, who boiled morphine with a chemical called acetic anhydride to discover what would happen. The result was a stronger chemical than morphine, called diacetylmorphine. Twenty years later, the Bayer drug company of Germany began synthesizing diacetylmorphine, under the supervision of chemist Felix Hoffmann. The drug was marketed as a pain reliever and cough medicine. It was sold under the name Heroin, probably a derivation of the German word *heroisch*, which means "heroic."

Early medical studies of heroin indicated it was safe. Doctors saw it as a potential treatment for morphine addiction and a safe medicine for coughs and pain, even in small children. According to the *Boston Medical and Surgical Journal,* "It [heroin] possesses many advantages over morphine. It's not hypnotic, and there's no danger of acquiring a habit."

Bayer's heroin was soon sold in more than 20 countries. It was available as a candy-like tablet, a water-soluble powder, and as an **elixir**.

As early as 1899, some doctors were warning that heroin users were becoming dependent on the drug. Soon, researchers found that heroin was even more addictive than morphine. After worldwide reports of addiction, Bayer stopped making heroin in 1913. The drug was soon outlawed around the world, with the United States formally banning it in 1924.

Heroin is sold illegally today. It is often found as a white or brown powder, or as a sticky black tar-like substance.

Opioid Pain Relievers Appear

During the twentieth century, new drugs were created in laboratories and intended to mimic the effects of opium-based drugs like morphine and codeine. These synthetic drugs were not directly derived from the opium poppy, so they were called opioids. Among the first were oxycodone, which was synthesized in 1917, and hydromorphone, which was first produced in 1922. Another was hydrocodone, which is a synthetic opioid with effects similar to codeine. It was first synthesized by a German pharmaceutical company, Knoll, in 1920. Later opioids included fentanyl, synthesized by Janssen Pharmecutica in 1949.

All of the opioids were effective painkillers. But due to their high potential for abuse, addiction, and overdose, opioids in general were usually prescribed only to cancer patients and people experiencing excruciating pain. This began to change in the late twentieth century, as pharmaceutical companies began actively working to inform doctors about the potential benefits of opioids. Supported by Big Pharma, organizations were created to advocate for the use of opioids to treat all sorts of pain, including chronic pain caused by arthritis and other conditions, and for acute pain caused by injuries.

In 1971, for example, the German pharmaceutical company Knoll created a new painkiller by combining the narcotic hydrocodone with the analgesic pain reliever acetaminophen. It marketed this drug under the brand name Vicodin. Before the company could begin selling the drug in the United States, it went through an approval process conducted by the Food and Drug Administration (FDA). Under FDA guidelines, hydrocodone is considered a Schedule II narcotic, similar to morphine, which means its

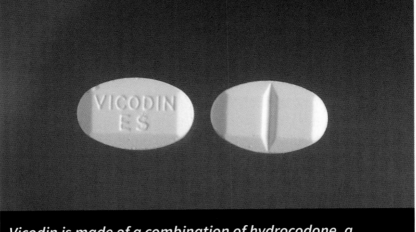

Vicodin is made of a combination of hydrocodone, a synthetic opiate, and acetaminophen, a non-steroidal pain reliever. It is considered to be highly addictive, and has a high potential for abuse.

use is strictly regulated. But because the company had added acetaminophen, Knoll was able to get Vicodin classified as an FDA Schedule III drug. Drugs in this category are thought to have a lower potential for addiction and abuse, and can be prescribed to treat a broader range of issues. US sales of Vicodin began in the late 1970s.

By the 1990s, as prescriptions for opioid painkillers became more common, abuse of Vicodin increased. Emergency room visits related to Vicodin dependency or overdose rose more than 500 percent between 1990 and 2002. Many people became addicted to Vicodin, including the rapper Eminem, pro football quarterback Brett Favre, and celebrity Nicole Richie. In 2009, a medical advisory panel advised the FDA to ban Vicodin, but the FDA did not agree. Vicodin is still prescribed and used to relieve pain.

Beginning an Epidemic

Experts from the Drug Enforcement Agency (DEA), the CDC, and US Surgeon General's office have agreed that 1996 marks the start of the opioid epidemic. That year, Purdue

Pharma spent $207 million to launch its new opioid painkiller, OxyContin. OxyContin is a timed-release pill containing a powerful opioid, oxycodone. The company claimed that each dose of the drug could relieve pain for up to twelve hours.

To promote the new drug, Purdue Pharma hired hundreds of salespeople. Some marketed the drug to the traditional customers for opioids: cancer clinics or pain specialists. But most of the new Purdue sales force focused on encouraging family doctors and general practitioners to prescribe OxyContin to their patients. They claimed that because the oxycodone was only released gradually over a twelve-hour period, the drug was safe and non-addictive.

Between 1996 and 2001, the company held more than forty conferences hosting over 5,000 doctors at resorts in Arizona, California, and Florida. The drug company paid the doctors' expenses paid to attend these conferences and learn more about OxyContin.

The company's investment paid off. In 1996, sales of OxyContin totaled $48 million. By 2000, OxyContin sales surpassed $1 billion. By 2002, almost 14 million OxyContin were being written and sales were almost $3 billion.

However, despite the company's claims OxyContin was not safe at all. The drug was highly addictive. Purdue Pharma's successful marketing campaign came at a terrible human cost—high rates of addiction, abuse, and easy availability to prescription drugs, which could be abused. By 2005, 2.1 million people were telling authorities that they had first used drugs illegally by trying prescription painkillers like OxyContin.

State and federal authorities investigated the company. In May 2007, Purdue Pharma and three of the company's top officials pled guilty to charges that they had misled doctors and patients about the danger of OxyContin addiction. A federal court in Virginia ruled that the company had to pay over

$634 million in fines and payments to patients who were injured by the medication, and Purdue's president, medical director, and lead attorney were ordered to pay more than $35 million in additional fines.

The federal court ruling did not prevent Purdue Pharma from continuing to sell OxyContin. By 2010, the drug was producing more than $3 billion in annual sales for Purdue Pharma. In addition, shortly after Purdue Pharma's guilty plea resulting in more than $600 million in fines and penalties, the company's owners opened a second drug company in Rhode Island called Rhodes Pharma. Rhodes Pharma began making and selling generic opioid painkillers. By 2016, Purdue and Rhodes Pharma together sold more than 14.4 million opioid prescriptions.

In recent years, additional lawsuits have been filed against Purdue Pharma and its owners, the Sackler family. By 2019, thirty-six states were suing Perdue Pharma over its deceptive marketing practices, and the company announced that it would no longer actively market OxyContin. However, Purdue continues to sell OxyContin, because it still brings in billions of dollars of revenue to the company each year.

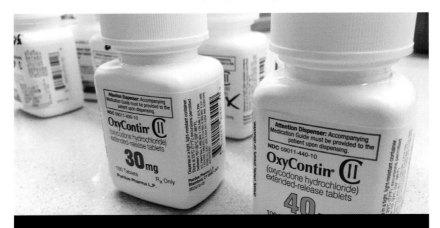

Most public health experts believe that the opioid epidemic in the United States started with the introduction of OxyContin in the late 1990s.

1. Where was laudanum available during the nineteenth century?
2. How many Civil War veterans became addicted to morphine?
3. Why did Purdue Pharma salespeople focus on family doctors when marketing OxyContin?

RESEARCH PROJECT

Using your school library or the internet, find out more about the Opium Wars of the nineteenth century. Write a two-page essay that briefly explains why the Opium Wars were fought, and how they were resolved. Conclude with a few paragraphs about whether the conflicts were right or wrong, using facts to support your opinion.

US Surgeon General Vivek Murthy speaks with a drug addict at the Wakefield Recovery Center in the Bronx, New York City.

WORDS TO UNDERSTAND

antagonist—a compound that opposes opioid drugs binding to opioid receptors.

complications—a secondary disease that results from an already existing one.

evidence-based—a type of treatment or care that has been studied and shown to be effective.

profits—the difference between the amount earned and the amount spent in buying, operating, or producing something.

CHAPTER 3

THE COST OF TREATMENT

Since the brain theory of addiction has been researched and understood, most treatment for opioid use disorders or opioid addiction includes medication-assisted treatment (MAT). Medications which help the body and brain to heal from long-term opioid use are similar to opioids but cause the body to reject opioids and begin to build its own natural pain relieving ability and ability to feel enjoyment and pleasure without opioid drugs.

Current drug treatment models include these medications along with counseling, therapy, self-help groups, and complementary and alternative medicine (CAM). People entering into medication-assisted treatment programs can spend anywhere from about $5,200 a year for buprenorphine, and $6,500 a year for methadone treatment to over $14,000 a year for naltrexone treatment. The National Institute on Drug Abuse has compared these costs to treatment for other chronic health conditions. Treatment for diabetes costs about $3,560 a year, and kidney disease, about $5,600 a year.

If people who are addicted to opioids continue to take the drugs with no treatment, costs are much higher on an individual basis. A study conducted by the *Boston Globe's* STAT website found that the average cost of hospital care for opioid overdoses rose from $58,500 to $92,400 between 2009 and 2015. Researchers evaluated more than 23 million people who were admitted to the hospital for opioid-related health emergencies the study period. More than 4 million of the patients were admitted to intensive care, which is much more expensive than the average cost of care.

In 2013, the NIDA reported that the total cost of medical care for opioid-related health problems was $78 billion. Only $2.8 billion of that total, or less than 3 percent, was spent on opioid addiction treatment.

The Cost to Taxpayers

The majority of states, most major cities, many counties, and many Native American tribes are suing the manufacturers of prescription opioids to recover the costs they have had to pay for emergency treatment, overdoses, and criminal prosecutions related to the opioid epidemic.

In addition to the direct health care costs for healthcare treatment for opioid addicts, indirect costs include the following problems, according to the National Institute on Drug Abuse (NIDA):

Related diseases like Hepatitis A and B and HIV/AIDS

Healthcare for addicted babies

Workplace injuries

Car accidents caused by people using opioids

Lost productivity at work

Criminal prosecutions

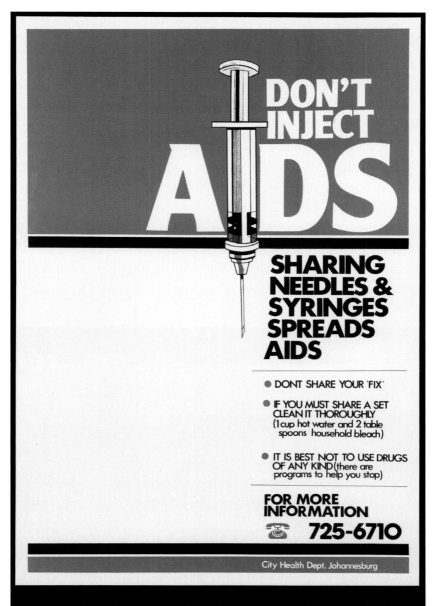

People who inject illegal heroin or other opioids are at risk of becoming infected with HIV/AIDS and hepatitis if they share needles with other drug users. This poster from the 1990s warns about the risks of AIDS and shared syringes.

According to attorney Mark Chalos, who works for a law firm that is counseling counties on how to prepare opioid-related lawsuits against pharmaceutical companies, "The costs build up slowly over time, but when our people really started to dig into the budgets, they realized the costs are more significant."

Middletown, Ohio, is a city of about 48,000 people with an annual budget of $30 million. It's a good example of a typical small American city. Every time the city's ambulance service responded to a call in which the emergency overdose reversal drug naloxone was administered, it cost the city about $1,140, according to a report from Middletown's city council. That means in 2016, when emergency responders answered over 900 overdose calls, the cost to taxpayers exceeded $1 million.

THE COST OF NALOXONE

Naloxone, sold under the brand name Narcan, is an emergency overdose reversal drug. It is an opioid **antagonist** which stops overdoses by restoring the brain's ability to control breathing and maintain a normal heart rate. Naloxone can be given in a nasal spray, by injection, or with a self-injection pen. Naloxone is a life-saving emergency medicine, not a drug that can help addicts to recover over the long term. In addition to first responders, some drug dealers provide Narcan to their customers. Narcan has cost Medicaid and Medicare over $140 million since 2014, according to a 2018 report from the US Senate Subcommittee on Homeland Security and Investigations.

Every call that ambulance crews make for opioid-related problems like accidental overdoses drains local government funds that could have been used for other purposes.

That is money that could have been better spent on improving roads and infrastructure or providing more services to low-income residents.

On a national level, the economic cost is staggering. Research group Altarum reported in 2018 that since the opioid epidemic began in the late 1990s, the overall cost to American society is over $1 trillion. The costs are still rising. Recently, the White House Council of Economic Advisers estimated that the annual cost of the epidemic was $500 billion.

Painkiller Use in the US

In 2017, the United Nations issued a report on the international use of opioids. It found that the United States uses 80 percent of the world's prescription pain drugs. On a per-capita basis, prescriptions were 50 percent higher than the second-place country, Germany. According to New York Special Narcotics Prosecutor Bridget Brennan, "We didn't develop an opioid epidemic until there was a huge surplus of opioids, which started with pharmaceutical drugs."

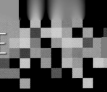
Many labor analysts now believe that opioid abuse and addiction is one of the reason that the United States has a lower labor force participation rate than all but one of the thirty-six countries in the Organization for Economic Co-Operation and Development (OECD). The OECD is composed of the world's most economically advanced countries. A 2016 report compiled by Princeton economist Alan Krueger found that nearly half of American men ages twenty-five to fifty-four were taking prescription painkillers every day. Krueger's research found that the decline in the US workforce corresponds with increased painkiller prescriptions between 1999 and 2015.

Purdue Pharma, the makers of OxyContin, is one of the companies that is being sued by state and local governments for its role in fueling the opioid crisis. The family that owns the company is believed to have earned over $4 billion in **profits** just from OxyContin between 2007 and 2017. Overall, the world's top eleven pharmaceutical companies earned $711 billion in profits between 2003 and 2012, according a public watchdog organization, Public Citizen. Not all of the companies' profits were from opioid medications. With an estimated public cost of $1 trillion between 1999 and 2018, the opioid epidemic has cost the public much more than pharmaceutical companies have earned profits.

The Cost of Addiction to Individuals

Recent studies have shown that three out of ten adults in the United States who are under age fifty and receiving Medicaid benefits are using prescription or illegal opioids. Medicaid is a program provided for people who are unemployed or low-income. Individuals have to earn less than 138 percent of the Federal Poverty Level to receive Medicaid. The majority of these people were employed at one time and lost their jobs as a result of drug addiction.

People who are already poor and use drugs face severe financial penalties. In addition to buying drugs, which can cost up to half a person's monthly income, drug addicts can be arrested and required to pay fines, court costs, and lawyer's fees. Drug addiction is associated with lower performance at work and at school. Many drug addicts eventually lose their jobs. Drugabuse.com's educational website points out that drugs will continue to affect someone's financial well-being even if they enter recovery. Being unemployed for several years will reduce Social Security and other retirement income later in life.

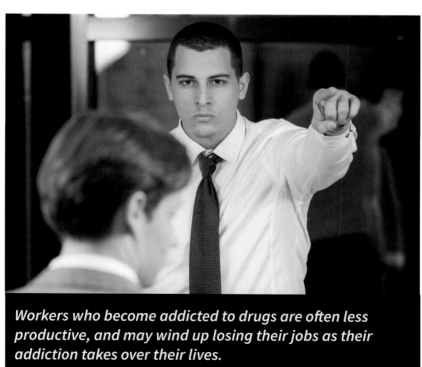

Workers who become addicted to drugs are often less productive, and may wind up losing their jobs as their addiction takes over their lives.

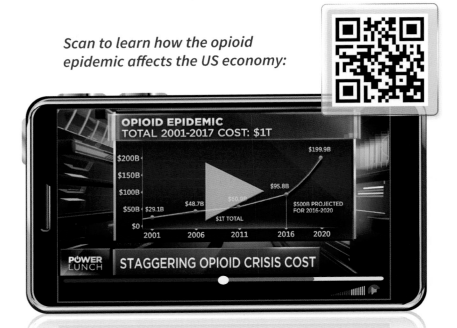

Scan to learn how the opioid epidemic affects the US economy:

If drug addicts use opioids and drive, they risk being arrested for driving while impaired. In previous generations, drunk driving was the most serious concern for drivers and law enforcement officers. According to the National Survey on Drug Use and Health, in 2017, 12.8 million people drove under the influence of drugs. Also, in 2017 for the first time, the number of fatal car accidents resulting from drugged driving bypassed the deadly crashes caused by drunk driving for the first time. Fines for drugged driving are the same or in some cases higher than those for drunk driving. At a minimum, drivers will lose their license for several months and pay fines and lawyer's fees totaling $5,000 to $10,000.

How Much Does Addiction Treatment Cost?

Treatment for opioid addiction can take several different forms and include several different phases. Inpatient treatment is a type of hospital stay. Patients go to a rehab center and receive treatment with medication that can help reduce withdrawal symptoms and cravings. They also receive counseling, have the opportunity to participate in support groups, and may have other types of therapy depending on the program. Whether or not a patient has insurance determines how much an individual will pay. The cost of twenty-eight-day residential treatment programs usually starts at about $2,000 for very basic program, and can be as high as $25,000 to $35,000 for luxury programs.

Because opioids cause physical dependency, withdrawal symptoms can be severe and at times, life-threatening. Medically supervised detox programs which include medication and round the clock medical care can cost anywhere from $250 to $800 a day. Before an opioid addict can enter rehab, they need to complete a detox program and be recovered enough to begin the next phase of their treatment.

Outpatient programs can come in two forms: intensive outpatient treatment and regular outpatient treatment. Other

Many hospitals, such as this Veterans Affairs medical center in Minneapolis, offer programs and facilities to treat people addicted to opioids or other drugs.

similar programs are called partial hospitalization or day hospitalization programs. In each of these programs, the addicted person attends organized treatment for a specific amount of time each day. Some partial hospitalization programs provide treatment for eight to ten hours a day, while regular outpatient programs usually meet for one to two hours a day, three days a week. These programs can cost as little as $500 a month, on up to $10,000 a month for luxury programs that provide food and recreation opportunities. Partial hospitalization usually costs between $250 and $350 a day.

Most people receive some assistance from insurance to pay for rehab programs. People who are very low income can apply for programs like Medicaid which can help to pay for care. Many communities also have not-for-profit drug rehab organizations that offer a sliding fee scale based on the ability to pay. Some programs are free of charge, particularly community-based programs. Finally, self-help and twelve-step groups are always free, like Narcotics Anonymous (NA) and Alcoholics Anonymous (AA). A person who uses opioids can attend AA meetings as well as NA meetings.

Narcotics Anonymous

One program that helps addicts recover from opioid addiction is Narcotics Anonymous. Narcotics Anonymous (NA) is a twelve-step organization founded in 1953 and it is free of charge. Twelve-step groups are either based on or inspired by Alcoholics Anonymous (AA), which provided a philosophy of twelve steps in individual recovery from substance abuse and addiction. NA doesn't focus on any particular drug, and it also includes people seeking recovery from alcohol abuse.

NA currently holds almost 67,000 regular meetings in 139 countries. The organization's First Step refers specifically to

Twelve Steps of
Narcotics Anonymous

1. We admitted that we were powerless over our addiction, that our lives had become unmanageable.

2. We came to believe that a Power greater than ourselves could restore us to sanity.

3. We made a decision to turn our will and our lives over to the care of God *as we understood Him.*

4. We made a searching and fearless moral inventory of ourselves.

5. We admitted to God, to ourselves, and to another human being the exact nature of our wrongs.

6. We were entirely ready to have God remove all these defects of character.

7. We humbly asked Him to remove our shortcomings.

8. We made a list of all persons we had harmed, and became willing to make amends to them all.

9. We made direct amends to such people wherever possible, except when to do so would injure them or others.

10. We continued to take personal inventory and when we were wrong promptly admitted it.

11. We sought through prayer and meditation to improve our conscious contact with God *as we understood Him,* praying only for knowledge of His will for us and the power to carry that out.

12. Having had a spiritual awakening as a result of these steps, we tried to carry this message to addicts, and to practice these principles in all our affairs.

This page from the Institutional Group Guide *for Narcotics Anonymous details the "twelve steps" of the addiction recovery process.*

"addiction." NA emphasizes the disease concept of addiction, and in its way, provided a precursor to the commonly accepted brain theory of addiction today. All "anonymous" recovery programs, including NA, are open to any person in need of recovery, regardless of their religious background, social status, gender, or nationality.

NA surveyed over 22,000 members in 2015 and found out that 59 percent of members were male and 41 percent female. Over 60 percent of members were employed full-time, and 25 percent of members had been sober over twenty years. Over 40 percent of members had been sober for more than five years.

Members reported that the biggest benefits of their participation in NA were improved family relationships and social connections. More than 70 percent also said they'd gotten stable employment and housing since joining and participating in NA.

According to NA, "Active addiction is marked by increased isolation and destruction of relationships," and over 90 percent of the organization's members reported being less isolated and having better relationships because they participated in NA.

Finding Treatment Programs

The US Department of Health and Human Services (HHS) reported more than 2.1 million people with opioid use disorder in 2017. Of this group, over 880,000 people used heroin. Over 11 million people misused prescription opioids in 2017 according to HHS, putting them at potential risk of addiction.

As of 2018, with White House Council of Economic Advisors reporting an estimated $500 billion cost of emergency care, lost work productivity, and unemployment, more treatment and prevention is clearly needed. Only about 10 percent of the 2.1 million people who have opioid use disorders (OUD) seek treatment, according to the Centers for Disease Control. The Harm Reduction Coalition has recommended that the federal government spend $100 billion more on opioid treatment and prevention, but the Department of Health and Human Services provided $1 billion in grants, only 1 percent of the recommendation.

The lack of funding provides some explanation for why nine out of ten people who are addicted to opioids don't seek treatment. There's no way to determine how many people try to get into a treatment program but are turned away due to lack of space. There are too few treatment programs available, especially in rural areas. In urban areas, treatment programs often have long waiting lists.

"In cities like Baltimore where there are fentanyl, heroin, and opioid problems, there's just not enough treatment centers," said Dr. Martin Makary, a physician at Johns Hopkins Hospital who also leads the Center for Opioid Research and Education (CORE).

Although government and healthcare organizations at all levels are working to expand treatment programs providing **evidenced-based** treatments like medication-assisted treatment

 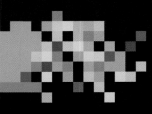

PREMATURE DEATHS

Average life expectancy declined in the United States for the third year in a row in 2018. Most health officials attribute the decline to the opioid epidemic. A 2018 report in the *Journal of American Medicine* found that opioid deaths cost 1.68 million person-years of life in 2016. The highest level of premature deaths occurred among young adults aged twenty-four to thirty-five, who could have expected to live many more years if they hadn't used opioids.

combined with cognitive-behavioral therapy (CBT), nine out of ten people who are addicted to opioids aren't getting the treatment they need.

The Cost to Increase Treatment Options

Medication-assisted treatment is an evidence-based treatment for opioid addiction that uses three different medications along with counseling and support groups. The treatment program helps patients to overcome opioid withdrawal symptoms and cravings while they develop healthy habits of recovery. The type of medication that is used affects the cost, which range from $5,980 per year to slightly more than $14,000 a year according to the National Institute on Drug Abuse (NIDA).

While there are many reports of the cost of emergency room visits, Narcan doses, and overdose deaths which add up to official estimates that the opioid epidemic cost the United States $500 billion in 2018, even the National Institute on Drug Abuse (NIDA) hasn't added up how much providing medication-assisted treatment would cost. With an estimated 2.1 million people with opioid use disorders (OUD) in the US, providing the lowest-cost MAT to every one of them adds up to $12.5 billion. Providing the highest-cost medication, naltrexone, along with counseling and other recovery supports to every opioid addict for a year would cost $29.6 billion.

These are very high amounts of money, but they are much lower than the current amounts that are being spent on law enforcement related to opioid overdoses, emergency room care, and long-term health treatment for opioid addicts. When lost work time and severe health **complications** from opioid use, including strokes and kidney failure are added in, the cost of treatment amounts to about 5 percent of what the United States currently spends on the opioid epidemic.

TEXT-DEPENDENT QUESTIONS

1. What are some reasons why many people with opioid use disorders don't seek treatment?
2. How much did Purdue Pharma earn in profit from OxyContin between 2007 and 2017?
3. What percentage of adults under age fifty and receiving Medicaid benefits are using prescription or illegal opioids?

RESEARCH PROJECT

Research more about the emergency overdose drug naloxone. Use government or reliable news websites that explain how the drug works. Look for ways that emergency and first responders use the drug. If you live in an area where Narcan has been provided to your school nurse or health office, look for occasions where has been used on someone having an overdose. Write a one-page essay about how naloxone can save lives and explain whether or not you think this drug will solve the opioid crisis or just keep it going. Include your sources at the end of the essay.

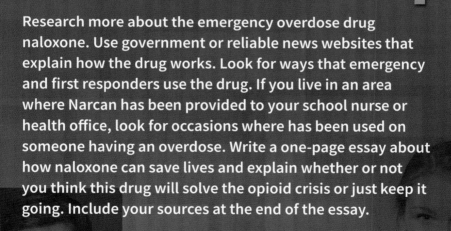

Addiction

For most drug users, the greatest barrier to treatment is their belief that they do not need help. Instead, they allow their addiction to control their lives.

WORDS TO UNDERSTAND

agonist—in pharmaceutical terms, a compound that binds to the body's receptors in the opioid system or other systems.

contingency— a provision for an unforeseen event or circumstance.

neurotransmitter—a chemical substance released by a nerve fiber in response to a nerve impulse.

relapse—a deterioration of recovery and return to substance use after a period of improvement.

voucher—a small printed piece of paper that can be exchanged for goods or services.

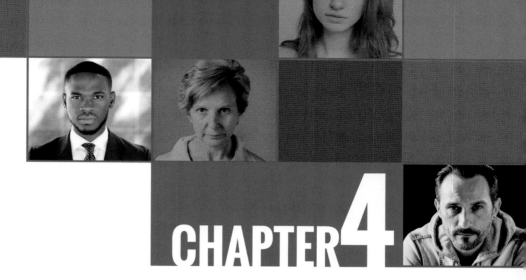

CHAPTER 4

HOW DOES OPIOID ADDICTION TREATMENT WORK?

In the nineteenth century, opioid addicts like British author Samuel Taylor Coleridge spent years under a doctor's care with little to no improvement in their addiction or health. People can also stop using opioids on their own and even quit "cold turkey," like former Green Bay Packer quarterback Brett Favre. Brett Favre credits the support he received from his family, teammates, and friends for helping him to break his addiction to Vicodin.

The part of quitting opioids where people usually need help involves withdrawal symptoms, cravings, dependency, and **relapse** triggers. Research has uncovered the way that opioids change the body and brain. The brain theory of addiction shows how these drugs distort our brain's chemical reward system, taking the place of normal, positive rewards that we usually get for doing healthy, positive things.

Quarterback Brett Favre began taking Vicodin in 1992, after he was injured in a football game. By 1996, Favre recognized that his addiction to the painkiller was affecting his life. He entered the Menninger Clinic, an inpatient treatment facility in Topeka, Kansas, and spent forty-six days there. Favre was able to change his life and resume his career. Six months after completing treatment, he led the Green Bay Packers to victory in Super Bowl XXXI.

People who are addicted to opioids don't have the same abilities to make decisions or analyze the rewards and risks of taking opioids as they did before they started taking the drug. The longer people use opioids, the greater the chance they will relapse if they try to quit on their own. Although addiction to opioids seems to be almost universally associated with weak willpower in the minds of many people, the truth is that the drugs themselves cause a cycle of dependency that leads to addiction in many cases. Just as people can't relieve severe pain on their own without pain medication, most people who have become addicted to opioids can't enter recovery and maintain it without treatment.

The National Institute on Drug Abuse (NIDA) and the Substance Abuse and Mental Health Services Administration (SAMHSA) both study evidence-based treatments for drug abuse. Opioid addiction has some unique qualities in the way that opioid drugs, both prescribed and illicit, influence the mind and body. The primary evidence-based treatment for opioid addiction is medication-assisted treatment combined with behavioral therapy and peer and family support.

What Is Opioid Dependency?

Opioids imitate the way that our body's own natural pain-relieving system provides relief in case of injuries. Taken over a long period of time, legal and illegal opioids change the way our body's opioid receptors respond. They limit the body's ability to respond to its own natural pain-relieving **neurotransmitters** and train opioid receptors to respond only to the drug. They also reduce our natural ability to produce "feel good" neurochemicals like endorphins.

Opioid drugs also cause our brains to produce artificially large amounts of dopamine, a natural "feel good" brain chemical. Dopamine that our bodies produce normally gives us the desire to keep doing activities that provide a reward, like getting an "A" on a test or working out at the gym. Dopamine can be responsible for most motivation that we have to do anything positive.

When opioid users take the drug, dopamine floods their brains. It is responsible for the "high" that opioid users get when they take the drug. The way opioids work for everybody leads to physical dependency. Dependency means that over time, a person needs to keep taking the drug in order to feel normal. If they stop taking opioids, they will suffer physical withdrawal symptoms, some of which can be very severe and even potentially life-threatening. Physical dependency combined with artificially increased dopamine that provides a chemical, false sense of "reward" can be a powerful combination that most opioid users struggle to overcome.

Everyone who takes opioid medication for more than a few days will have some degree of dependency. Addiction and dependency are different. Not every person who takes opioids becomes addicted, but every person who uses opioids for a long time will become physically dependent on them.

How Does Withdrawal Affect Treatment?

Once a long-term opioid user stops taking the drugs, they will experience withdrawal symptoms. Early withdrawal symptoms are like a cold or flu, including watery eyes and a runny nose. Other early symptoms can include excessive sweating, muscle pains, anxiety, and difficulty sleeping. Because opioids depress heart and breathing rates, people in early withdrawal will experience faster heart rates and breathing, as well as nausea, diarrhea, and vomiting. Withdrawal can also cause muscle cramps and dilated pupils, along with strong drug cravings.

Withdrawal symptoms usually begin about twelve to thirty hours after the last use of opioids. The symptoms can last between four and ten days.

Treatment programs for opioid use disorders always begin with detox programs that range from a few days to a few weeks. Medically supervised detox programs help to reduce the discomfort of withdrawal and protect people in early recovery. Medications including naltrexone and buprenorphine help to reduce withdrawal symptoms and cravings. Even after they have stopped taking opioids and entered recovery, some people experience post-acute

To learn how MAT helps to overcome opioid addiction, scan here:

withdrawal syndrome (PAWS). PAWS can produce symptoms for months after some people stop taking opioids that include depression, anxiety, disturbed sleep, tiredness, and poor decision-making ability.

Replacing One Drug With Another

Medication-assisted treatment (MAT) is an evidence-based treatment for opioid addiction that provides daily doses of opioid antagonists or partial antagonists that help to relieve withdrawal symptoms. Provided over time during an addicted person's recovery, MAT drugs can support the brain and body's ability to heal and build its ability to respond to dopamine produced naturally. MAT helps people to heal from the changes that opioids cause during prolonged use.

Some critics of MAT say that using drugs like naltrexone, buprenorphine, and methadone simply replace one drug with another, even though the replacement drugs don't cause

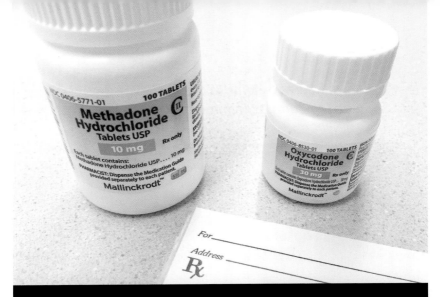

The drug methadone relieves the uncomfortable symptoms of withdrawal without the potent "high" of heroin or painkillers. It is considered the original MAT drug.

a "high" effect like addictive prescription or illegal opioids. According to the National Institute on Drug Abuse (NIDA), MAT drugs are "prescribed or administered under monitored, controlled conditions and are safe and effective for treating opioid addiction when used as directed."

Only about 20 percent of people with substance use disorders are receiving medications to help them maintain their recovery, but prescriptions for the drugs used in medication-assisted treatment are on the rise. Three drugs are commonly used to support recovery from opioid addiction: methadone, buprenorphine, and naltrexone.

Methadone is the oldest MAT drug. It was invented in 1939 and is an opioid **agonist**, which allows it to reduce withdrawal symptoms and drug cravings. Methadone doesn't cause a feeling of being "high." It is usually used for heroin addiction, but it may also benefit other people with opioid use disorders. Methadone can only be offered at methadone clinics. It can't be used with a prescription for home or individual use.

Buprenorphine is a partial opioid "agonist" which binds to endogenous opioid receptors and helps to reduce drug cravings and withdrawal symptoms. It is available as an injection, a tablet, or a transdermal patch. Some types of buprenorphine can be implanted or injected once a month. Unlike methadone, buprenorphine can be prescribed by a doctor for home use or dispensed in a doctor's office or clinic.

Naltrexone is an opioid "antagonist" which means prevents opioids from binding to opioid receptors. One of the brand names of naltrexone is Vivitrol. Vivitrol can be injected, providing effects for up to two weeks. Vivitrol also has some benefits for other types of drug addiction and alcohol dependency.

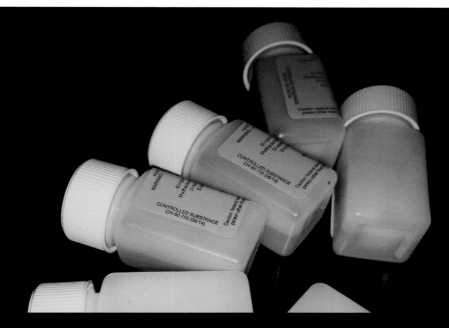

A person who is trying to break addiction to opioids under a doctor's supervision may be eligible to receive daily doses of methadone at a local clinic. The methadone is often dispensed as an orange-colored liquid. However, methadone clinics are sometimes controversial, as homeowners may be concerned that they will draw undesirable drug addicts to their neighborhoods.

More than Drug Treatment

Medication-assisted treatment uses drugs like methadone or buprenorphine help addicts to overcome physical withdrawal symptoms and cravings that result from the changes that long-term use of opioids has made in their central nervous system. The drugs alone don't provide the human support and coping skills that addicts need to maintain their recovery, prevent relapse, and avoid triggers that could lead them back into opioid use.

The National Institute on Drug Abuse (NIDA) recommends that medication-assisted treatment be combined with

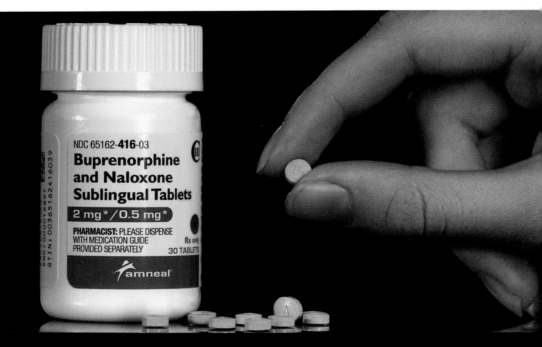

Unlike methadone, buprenorphine and naloxone are sometimes prescribed for patients to take at home. While it was originally developed as a MAT drug, researchers are currently investigating whether these drugs can also provide a safer alternative to conventional opioids for managing chronic pain.

counseling and community and family support for a better chance of ongoing recovery. Because opioid addiction is a chronic disease, it can never be completely cured. Addicted people can and do enter recovery and maintain it for their entire lifetime.

Treatment plans for opioid addicts should be individualized, and they should also reflect any additional problems that could cause complications or be risks for relapse. Treatment options for opioid addiction include residential treatment, which can range from twenty-eight days to several months, and outpatient treatment, which takes place in the community. Employed people often seek outpatient treatment because they can continue to work while attending treatment in the evenings or on weekends.

What Are Co-occurring Disorders?

Opioid use can affect mental and physical health in many different ways. Opioid users also may suffer from health conditions which cause pain, and which led them to take opioids in the first place. Some opioid addicts have pre-existing conditions, including:

- Back or joint injuries and pain
- Osteoarthritis (OA) and Rheumatoid Arthritis (RA)
- Fibromyalgia and other long-term pain conditions
- Cancer pain
- HIV/AIDS
- Hepatitis C

Opioid influence on neurotransmitters like dopamine leads to increased depression and anxiety. Depression is frequently a co-occurring disorder diagnosed along with opioid use disorder (OUD). Other co-occurring mental health disorders which some people can experience include anxiety disorders, bipolar disorders, obsessive-compulsive disorder (OCD), post-traumatic stress disorder (PTSD), and schizophrenia.

When people with OUD seek treatment for their addiction to opioids, they should also be assessed for co-occurring disorders. If they have an underlying condition that causes severe pain, they will find it very difficult to recover if their pain prevents them from activities of daily living as well as doing without opioids. The NIDA recommends a broad range of treatment options for physical and mental health co-occurring disorders.

Treatment programs have developed to treat people with opioid addiction and co-occurring disorders, but like treatment programs in general, they often have long waiting lists or are difficult for people to access.

Helpful Therapies

Behavioral therapy is an integral part of opioid addiction treatment. Although medication can help to relieve cravings and withdrawal symptoms, opioid addicts have learned behaviors that support their addiction. They usually have to re-learn healthy behaviors that support their relationships with family and friends and help to prevent relapse.

Social isolation is a feature of nearly all types of addiction. Opioid addicts eventually come to the point where they have severed all ties with people who don't use drugs. They may have lost their job, moved out of their family home, and gone through a divorce.

Group therapy in opioid addiction treatment programs often focuses on helping addicts to rebuild human relationships that don't center on drugs and drug-taking.

Counseling and group therapy are important elements of addiction recovery programs.

Several different types of behavioral therapy have been developed over the past thirty years. According to the NIDA, each of the following types of behavioral therapy can help people recover from substance abuse:

Cognitive-Behavioral Therapy (CBT): CBT began as a technique to help people stop abusing alcohol. Now it is used for opioid addiction and addictions to other drugs including marijuana, cocaine, and methamphetamines. CBT helps people in recovery to recognize triggers for their drug use, and to develop strategies to cope with the triggers when they experience them. CBT also helps people to develop alternative, healthy behaviors, avoid triggering situations, and develop ways to overcome cravings.

Community Reinforcement Plus Vouchers (CRA): The Community Reinforcement Approach (CRA) is a formal intensive 24-week outpatient program that was originally developed to help people to overcome an addiction to alcohol and cocaine. Opioid addicts can use the Therapeutic Educational System (TES) which is similar to the original CRA program. In each program, counseling is combined with drug testing. Participants receive **vouchers** for each clean drug test, which they can use to buy clothing, food, or other desirable products. The TES program also includes help to develop communication skills and sober social activities and recreation.

Contingency Management Interventions/Motivation Incentives: In use with programs treating several different types of addiction, including opioids, **contingency** management interventions provide vouchers that can be exchanged for desirable food items or products. Heroin addicts have been successful in recovering using a combination of contingency management intervention vouchers, methadone medication-assisted treatment and inpatient or outpatient counseling and support.

Types of Opioid Addiction Treatment

Opioid addicts can receive residential treatment or outpatient treatment. Residential treatment can range from a hospital setting where intensive, medically monitored detoxification is provided twenty-four hours a day to long-term sober living homes, where residents are responsible for their own sobriety and live among other addicts who are also in recovery.

Residential treatment programs can vary from a few days of acute hospital-based detox to sober living homes where people can stay for six months, twelve months, or longer. Long-term residential treatment is usually highly structured.

Residents learn how to cope with life without opioids. Some residential treatment programs are located in rural areas and include enrichment and healing programs in addition to group and individual therapy or twelve-step support groups like Narcotics Anonymous or Alcoholics Anonymous. Enrichment and healing programs that some recovering addicts have benefited from include equine (horse) therapy, art therapy, music therapy, yoga, and outdoor activities like hiking, skiing, and running.

Some residential treatment programs are gender-specific, because the recovery needs of men and women are different. Programs for co-occurring disorders and opioid addiction also include specific types of counseling, therapy, and medical treatment to help people with HIV/AIDS, chronic pain conditions, and depression.

HORSE THERAPY HELPS ADDICTS

Horse therapy has helped autistic children who can't speak learn to communicate better and it has also helped people who are recovering from opioid addiction. Equine-assisted therapy helps people who are struggling with addiction to learn how to communicate better by communicating with their therapy horse. Experts say that 90 percent of human communication is non-verbal, and by riding and working with horses, addicted people can gain a better understanding of and ability to cope with nonverbal communication in their lives.

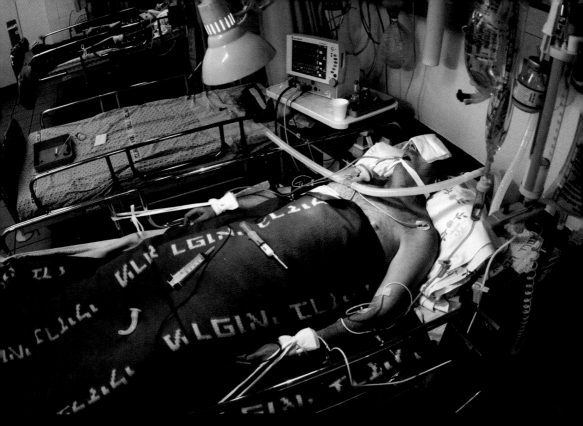

Anesthesia-assisted rapid opioid detoxification (ROD) is an effective but controversial method of getting addicts off drugs in the short term. It was developed in the 1980s, but today most medical experts recommend against using ROD treatments.

Outpatient treatment programs for opioid addiction often include a medication-assisted treatment component along with individual and group counseling and therapy. Similar to residential treatment programs, outpatient treatment can include additional therapies and enrichment to build sober living skills and avoid triggers for relapse. Outpatient programs can meet for a few hours two or three days a week to half-day programs or all-day programs. All-day outpatient programs are also sometimes called partial hospitalization programs or PHP.

TEXT-DEPENDENT QUESTIONS

1. Why can't most people enter and maintain recovery without treatment?
2. What is opioid dependency?
3. How does withdrawal affect treatment?

RESEARCH PROJECT

Research online whether your community has residential drug treatment programs, outpatient drug treatment programs, or a combination of both. Refer to your local or county health department website to discover which programs a person addicted to opioids could access. How many programs accept private insurance payments or public funds like Medicaid? Does your community have treatment programs that are either free of charge or based on the ability to pay? Write a one-page report about the information you find for treatment resources in your community. Be sure to explain what a person who is addicted to opioids in your community can do to recover. Include the sources you found at the end of your report.

In recent years government officials have attempted to educate doctors and the public about the danger of opioid painkiller abuse. Here, officials from the Drug Enforcement Administration speak at a conference encouraging doctors to find alternative therapies for chronic pain to reduce the number of opioid prescriptions.

WORDS TO UNDERSTAND

antidepressants—drugs that relieve symptoms of depression (antidepressants are not opioid drugs).

callous—having an insensitive and cruel disregard for others.

recovery—a return to a normal state of health, mind, or strength.

relapse—in someone suffering a disease, a deterioration after a period of improvement.

CHAPTER 5

THE LONG-TERM OUTLOOK

Most economic, social, and public health experts believe that the opioid epidemic will continue to get worse before it gets better. The illegal sale of powerful, potentially deadly opioids like fentanyl and sufentanil has contributed to more overdose deaths. Doctors have become more aware of the dangers of overprescribing opioids for pain. Prescriptions are down, but the use of some opioid drugs like tramadol continues to increase.

At a cost of approximately $500 billion a year, the opioid epidemic represents approximately 2.5 percent of the United States GDP, which totaled $20.4 trillion in 2018. The epidemic is the primary reason that US life expectancy has decreased every year since 2015. Drug overdoses are the leading cause of death for Americans under age 50, and they overtook car crashes as the most common cause of accidental death in 2017.

As of April 2019, more than forty states had filed lawsuits against the makers of prescription opioids to try to get

New Yorkers march to raise awareness about opioid addiction, and seek funding for naloxone and overdose-prevention programs.

compensation for money they've spent on emergency treatment for opioid overdoses, law enforcement costs, loss of citizen life, and the costs of opioid-caused medical treatment. The two companies most frequently named in the lawsuits are Insys, which makes a fentanyl patch called Subsys, and Purdue Pharma, the makers of OxyContin, a time-release form of oxycodone, which is up to two times stronger than morphine. In addition to states, many counties and cities have joined in the opioid lawsuits, which allege that drug makers undertook many deceptive, dangerous, and illegal practices in order to sell as many of their opioid drugs as possible.

Most people are now aware that opioids are dangerous. Fewer people know that if the drugs are used for longer than a few days, the chance of addiction increases. They also don't know that some groups of people, including "opioid naïve" people who've never taken opioids before, the elderly, and veterans, are more vulnerable to addiction than others.

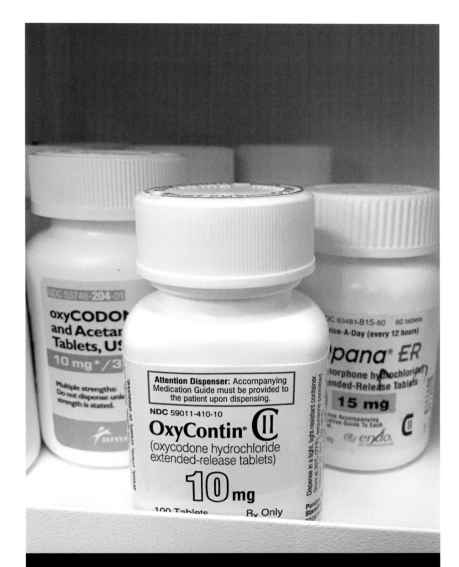

In recent years, OxyContin maker Purdue Pharma has been targeted with state lawsuits due to the company's deceptive marketing practices. In March 2019 the company settled one case with the state of Oklahoma for $270 million. At that time, hundreds of other lawsuits were still wending their way through the courts.

Awareness of medication-assisted treatment is increasing, but many people with opioid use disorders continue to think they can quit on their own and don't need any type of help or counseling.

Increased treatment is a clear solution for the 2.1 million people who are addicted to opioids. Prevention can help others to avoid becoming addicted in the future, including a reduction in the prescription of opioid painkillers. Finding alternatives for pain treatment will also help to reduce the epidemic and improve public health in the future.

Getting a Chance to Recover

One of the hallmarks of opioid addiction is the fact that addicts think they can quit any time they want. They may make a plan to quit every day, but that plan fails without help and support.

Actress Jamie Lee Curtis became addicted to prescription painkillers after a surgical procedure. It took her ten years to break her addiction.

"Quitting heroin was my plan every night when I went to sleep," said former heroin user Brian Rinker. "But when morning came, I'd rarely last an hour, let alone the day." When Brian first went to a detox facility, he was only able to stay for an hour before he had to leave to get more opioids. Brian's withdrawal symptoms included body aches, diarrhea, nausea, and cold sweats. He felt anxious, sick and depressed.

After moving to his parents' house because his addiction meant he couldn't work, Brian was forced to go without opioids. He spent three days and nights locked in his room, unable to sleep, frequently vomiting and suffering other withdrawal symptoms. He became able to walk around the house after the three days, and after two weeks, he had recovered enough awareness to go to a sober living home. After living in the sober living house for months, Brian had enough experience to stay off heroin. When he wrote his withdrawal and recovery experiences for Kaiser Health News, he hadn't used heroin for ten years.

People who are addicted to opioids have similar rates of relapse to people who have high blood pressure, asthma, and diabetes, according to studies conducted by the Centers for Disease Control. For example, a person with high blood pressure has symptoms which are eight out of ten before entering treatment, and they reduce their symptoms to two out of ten during treatment. After treatment is completed, the person with high blood pressure returns to older health habits, and their symptoms typically increase to six out of ten on a scale of one to ten. The treatment is considered successful in this case, because the person experienced a reduction in their high blood pressure although they didn't eliminate it completely.

According to the National Institute on Drug Abuse (NIDA), people who are addicted to opioids have a very similar pattern of improvement and relapse when they participate in treatment, yet in the case of opioid addiction, the treatment is considered a "failure." NIDA says that the attitudes of the public, addicted people, and healthcare professionals need to change, regarding both chronic health conditions and treatment similarly.

If opioid addicts can complete a thirty-day treatment program, they have a greater chance of success in avoiding relapses later on, but the condition is chronic and lifelong. So far, there is no cure for opioid addiction.

Helpful Practices for Recovery

Based on evidence from thousands of people who received treatment, the National Institute on Drug Abuse recommends a combination of medication-assisted treatment and behavioral treatment to help opioid addicts to recover. Behavioral treatment can include psychotherapy, including cognitive-behavioral therapy and group counseling. Groups like Narcotics Anonymous (NA) and Alcoholics Anonymous (AA) provide opportunities for self-help that can prevent relapse. As long as addicts have the opportunity to complete detox to overcome withdrawal symptoms, they can benefit from a combination of MAT, counseling, and self-help groups.

Even if addicts suffer a relapse and return to drug use, they can still re-enter recovery. Some people have relapsed dozens of times before achieving a lasting recovery without using opioids. The *Journal of the American Medical Association* reports that relapse rates for all substance use disorders range between 40 and 60 percent. According to the National Institute on Drug Abuse, relapse rates for people who need to lose weight to improve diabetes or high blood pressure are 50 to 70 percent.

Scan here to learn how a woman beat opioid addiction:

Joy Haywood
Peer Recovery Coach
Johns Hopkins Bayview Medical Center

NIDA reports that only about 21 percent of people who receive treatment for opioid use disorders receive medication-assisted treatment, which has been proven to increase success rates. Medicare won't pay for some MAT therapies like methadone, while some insurance companies won't pay for other medications like buprenorphine or naltrexone. Buprenorphine is an effective medication-assisted treatment drug, but it can only be provided to a limited number of patients per physician, and the doctors must be licensed. States are working to license more doctors to be qualified to provide buprenorphine to their patients. Currently, doctors licensed to provide buprenorphine are limited to 100 patients. A federal law is under consideration to allow them to treat up to 275 patients at a time.

If people suffer an overdose and receive emergency medical treatment, they seek additional treatment and recovery on their own if they receive buprenorphine in the emergency room before they're discharged. Their positive experience with the medication seems to encourage them to take action on their own. Addicts in prison who receive medication-assisted treatment and counseling while they are imprisoned are much more successful in avoiding relapses after they return to the community than addicts who receive no treatment or help while in jail.

Alternatives to Opioids

Now that the dangers of opioids have been revealed and so many people have overdosed and become addicted, doctors are seeking alternatives to relieve pain more safely. Some medications that have been overlooked include NSAIDs, or non-steroidal anti-inflammatory drugs like Advil and Motrin. These drugs are not addictive. A study published in the *Journal of the American Medical Society* found that

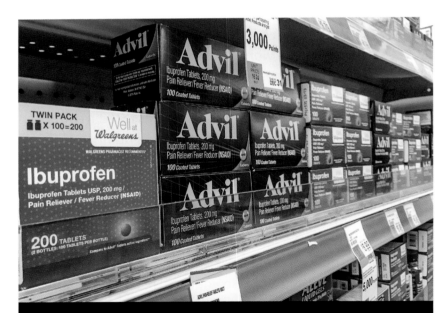

Non-steroidal anti-inflammatory drugs (NSAIDs) such as ibuprofen and acetaminophen can be used to treat pain without the addictive potential of opioids.

medications like Motrin are as good as opioids—and in some cases, better than opioids—at relieving pain from back injuries and arthritis pain. After six months, patients in the *JAMA* study reported less pain than comparison patients with the same conditions did after taking opioids.

Tricyclic antidepressants are older medications for depression that were discovered in the 1950s. They can relieve depression and pain. These medications can have side effects and reactions with some common other antidepressants, but if people aren't taking other medications that could have negative interactions, they may have reduced pain of they take tricyclic antidepressants like Elavil, Anafranil, and Sinequan.

The American Society of Anesthesiologists also recommend some non-drug therapies to relieve chronic pain. Their recommendations include:

Physical therapy: physical therapy and rehabilitation after injuries or surgery includes exercises that can strengthen muscles or improve mobility. Ultrasound treatment, whirlpool treatment and water therapy, and deep muscle massages are other physical therapies that provide pain relief.

Acupuncture: although some traditional Western medical practitioners still mock acupuncture, studies have shown it can relieve pain effectively. Acupuncture is a traditional form of Asian medicine which involves needles that are placed in different locations around the body. The needles interrupt and change nerve signals, resulting in pain relief.

Local anesthetics or steroid injections: Injections of anesthetic or anti-inflammatory drugs into painful areas can relieve pain.

In April 2019, the state legislature of West Virginia passed a bill that authorized the use of a special type of acupuncture, called auricular acudetox, to ease opioid withdrawal symptoms. Auricular acudetox involves the placement of acupuncture needles around the ear. Auricular acudetox has been used since the 1970s as part of drug treatment programs. The procedure is considered safe, although critics argue that independent scientific studies have not yet confirmed its effectiveness.

Additional therapies for pain relief that don't involve taking opioid drugs include hypnosis/hypnotherapy, and biofeedback. Biofeedback helps people to train themselves to respond to pain and reduce it using their body's own natural pain-fighting abilities. Sadly, these pain-fighting abilities are the very abilities that opioid drugs "hijack" and reduce if they are used over an extended period of time.

None of the suggested non-drug treatments for pain are addictive or would result in overdoses or a need for increased amounts of opioid drugs.

Ending the Epidemic

According to the Centers for Disease Control, about 3.3 million people misuse opioids, either prescription drugs, or drugs they purchase on the street, like fentanyl and heroin. Many people don't even try to seek treatment for their opioid addiction because they are ashamed and blame themselves for having weak willpower.

Opioid lawsuits are now revealing that unscrupulous drug companies like Purdue Pharma encouraged false beliefs about opioid addiction, including blaming individuals for the opioid epidemic.

Massachusetts' lawsuit against Purdue Pharma and its owners, the Sackler family, has revealed how they manipulated the opinions of healthcare providers and the public to sell more opioid prescription pills. When sales of OxyContin declined after Purdue Pharma paid a government fine of over $630 million in 2007, company president Richard Sackler blamed people addicted to opioids, not the medication itself. "We have to hammer on the abusers in every way possible," he told sales representatives. "They are the culprits and the problem. They are reckless criminals."

At the same time, Sackler, a medical doctor and opioid expert, was developing opioid-related drugs that could be used for medication-assisted treatment of addiction.

Physical therapy can help to relieve chronic pain in older patients by strengthening muscles and improving flexibility.

State and local governments are spending hundreds of millions of dollars to combat street drugs like heroin or help people who have suffered opioid overdoses. In a small town like Middletown, Ohio, the city is spending over $1 million of its $30 million budget responding to emergency overdose calls.

Although the federal government provided $1 billion for new opioid addiction treatment programs in 2018, the estimated need ranges between $12 and $24 billion. People living in rural areas must sometimes travel over a hundred miles for outpatient treatment, and often must go to other states to enter a residential treatment program.

Pharmaceutical company profits from opioid drugs have been substantial and may have exceeded $300 billion during the course of the opioid epidemic, but even these company profits are much less than the $1 trillion that economic forecasters like Altarum, a non-profit research and consulting firm, estimate that the epidemic has cost the general public.

Education and medicine have improved greatly since the introduction of morphine and heroin in the nineteenth century. Americans are more aware of the danger of dependency and addiction that opioids carry. Most medical professionals now recommend ways to relieve pain that include non-pharmaceutical approaches. When opioids are prescribed, the term is often limited to seven days or fewer, making it less likely that patience will develop a dependence. The solution to the opioid epidemic will no doubt involve looking beyond pain relief and toward other ways of healing the injuries and diseases that cause chronic pain.

TEXT-DEPENDENT QUESTIONS

1. What is the relapse rate for people who are addicted to opioids?
2. What are some practices that can help with recovery from addiction?
3. How can NSAIDs serve as an alternative to opioids?

RESEARCH PROJECT

Using your school library or the internet, find stories of young adults or teenagers who recovered from addiction to heroin or prescription opioids. You will find some stories that do not have a happy ending and other stories where the teens recovered and are living healthy, drug-free lives. Choose two of the stories and compare their recovery journeys in a one-page essay. Include your sources at the end of the paper.

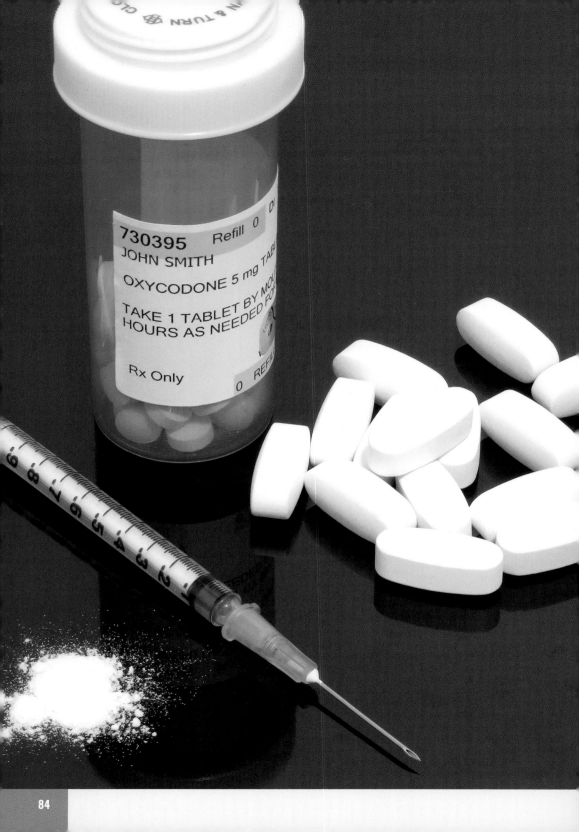

730395   Refill 0

JOHN SMITH

OXYCODONE 5 mg TAB

TAKE 1 TABLET BY MOU
HOURS AS NEEDED FO

Rx Only

CHAPTER NOTES

CHAPTER 1

p. 8: "During that time …" Alison, quoted in Kayla Adler, "I Was One Of The Top Doctors In My Field. I Was Also An Opioid Addict." *Marie Claire* (February 25, 2019). https://www.marieclaire.com/health-fitness/a26443838/top-doctor-opioid-addict/

p. 12: "Brain abnormalities …" Thomas R. Kosten and Tony P. George, "The Neurobiology of Opioid Dependence: Implications for Treatment," *Addiction Science and Clinical Practice* (July 2002). https://www.ncbi.nlm.nih.gov/pmc/articles/PMC2851054/

p. 15: "Nearly all addicted individuals …" National Institute on Drug Abuse, "Principles of Drug Addiction Treatment: A Research Guide (Third Edition)," (January 2018). https://www.drugabuse.gov/publications/principles-drug-addiction-treatment-research-based-guide-third-edition/frequently asked-questions/can-person-become-addicted-to-medications

p. 19: "I began using OxyContin …" Amanda, quoted in "Opioids Don't Discriminate: Stories of Addiction," Colorado Office of Behavioral Health (accessed May 2019). http://liftthelabel.org/stories/

p. 20: "women often use drugs …" National Institute on Drug Abuse, "Sex and Gender Differences in Substance Use," (July 2018). https://www.drugabuse.gov/publications/research-reports/substance-use-in-women/sex-gender-differences-in-substance-use

CHAPTER 2

p. 27: "I have in this one dirty business …" Samuel Taylor Coleridge, quoted in Claire Cock-Starkey, "The Lure of Laudanum, the Victorians' Favorite Drug," Mental Floss (November 29, 2016). http://mentalfloss.com/article/89268/lure-laudanum-victorians-favorite-drug

p. 30: "Maimed and shattered survivors …" Horace B. Day, *The Opium Habit* (New York: Harper and Brothers, 1868). https://www.fulltextarchive.com/pdfs/The-Opium-Habit.pdf

CHAPTER NOTES

p. 30: "Of all the nations of the world …" Hamilton Wright, quoted in "Heroin, Morphine, and Opiates," History.com (August 21, 2018). https://www.history.com/topics/crime/history-of-heroin-morphine-and-opiates

p. 32: "It [heroin] possesses many advantages …" *Boston Medical and Surgical Journal*, quoted in Richard Askwith, "How Aspirin Turned Hero," *Sunday Times* (September 13, 1998). https://www.opioids.com/heroin/heroinhistory.html

CHAPTER 3

p. 42: "The costs build up slowly …", Mark Chalos, quoted in Liz Farmer, "How Much Is the Opioid Crisis Costing Governments?" *Governing* (February 7, 2018). https://www.governing.com/topics/finance/gov-cost-opioid-crisis-governments.html

p. 43: "We didn't develop an opioid … " Bridget G. Brennan, quoted in Claire Felter, "The US Opioid Epidemic," Council On Foreign Relations (January 17, 2019). https://www.cfr.org/backgrounder/us-opioid-epidemic

p. 50: "active addiction …" Narcotics Anonymous, "Information About Narcotics Anonymous," (accessed May 2019). https://www.na.org/admin/include/spaw2/uploads/pdf/PR/InfoAboutNA_Nov2018.pdf

p. 51: "In cities like Baltimore …" Martin Makary, quoted in Alex Kacik, "Variety of Factors Drive Wide Variation in Opioid Treatment across the US," *Modern Healthcare* (August 11, 2018). https://www.modernhealthcare.com/article/20180811/NEWS/180819993/variety-of-factors-drive-wide-variation-in-opioid-treatment-across-the-u-s

CHAPTER 4

p. 60: "prescribed or administered …" National Institute on Drug Abuse, "Principles of Drug Addiction Treatment: A Research-Based Guide," (January 2018). https://www.drugabuse.gov/publications/principles-drug-addiction-treatment-research-based-guide-third-edition/frequently asked-questions/use-medications-methadone-buprenorphine

CHAPTER 5

p. 75: "quitting heroin was my plan …" Brian Rinker, "Commentary: What 'Dope Sick' Really Feels Like," *Chicago Tribune* (February 15, 2019). https://www.chicagotribune.com/lifestyles/health/sc-hlth-what-detox-feels-like-0306-story.html

p. 81: "We have to hammer on …" Richard Sackler, quoted in *Commonwealth of Massachusetts v. Purdue Pharma L.P. et. al*, (January 31, 2019). https://www.documentcloud.org/documents/5715954-Massachusetts-AGO-Amended-Complaint-2019-01-31.html

abstinence—to refrain from alcohol or drug use.

analgesic—any member of a class of drugs used to achieve analgesia, or relief from pain.

antagonist—a substance that counteracts the effects of another drug, by interacting with receptors in the brain to prevent drugs from activating the receptor and causing physical or psychological effects.

cardiovascular system—the system consisting of the heart and blood vessels. It delivers nutrients and oxygen to all cells in the body.

central nervous system—the system consisting of the nerves in the brain and spinal cord. These are greatly affected by opiates and opioids.

cerebellum—a part of the brain that helps regulate posture, balance, and coordination. It is also involved in the processes of emotion, motivation, memory, and thought.

chronic condition—a medical condition that persists for a long time (at least three months or more).

craving—an intense desire for a substance, also called "psychological dependence."

dependence—a situation that occurs when opiates or opioids are used so much that the user's body adapts to the drug and only functions normally when the drug is present. When the user attempts to stop using the drug, a physiologic reaction known as withdrawal syndrome occurs.

detoxification—medical treatment of a drug addict or alcoholic, intended to rid the patient's bloodstream of the psychoactive substance. The addict is usually required to abstain from the drug or alcohol. Also known as "detox," or "managed withdrawal."

dopamine—a brain chemical, classified as a neurotransmitter, found in regions of the brain that regulate movement, emotion, motivation, and reinforcement of rewarding behavior. Dopamine release in reward areas of the brain is caused by all drugs to which people can become addicted.

epidemic—a widespread occurrence of a disease or illness in a community at a particular time.

intravenous—drug delivery through insertion of a needle into a vein.

intranasal—drug delivery via inhalation through the nose.

naloxone—an antagonist that blocks opioid receptors in the brain, so that they are not activated by opioid drugs. Because it can reverse the problem of opiate intoxication, it is often used to treat overdoses of opioids, such as heroin, fentanyl, or painkillers like oxycodone or hydrocodone.

neuron—a unique type of cell found in the brain and throughout the body that specializes in the transmission and processing of information. Also called a "nerve cell." opiates—a drug that is derived directly from the poppy plant, such as opium, heroin, morphine, and codeine.

opioids—synthetic drugs that affect the body in a similar way as opiate drugs. The opioids include oxycodone, hydrocodone, fentanyl, and methadone.

overdose—the use of any drug in such an amount that serious physical or mental effects occur, including permanent brain damage, coma, or death. The lethal dose of a particular drug can varies depending on the strength of the drug as well as the individual who is taking it.

relapse—a return to drug use or drinking after a period of abstinence, often accompanied by a recurrence of drug dependence.

self-medication—the use of a drug to lessen the negative effects of stress, anxiety, or other mental disorders without the guidance of a health care provider. Self-medication may lead to addiction and other drug-related problems.

withdrawal—a syndrome of often painful physical and psychological symptoms that occurs when someone stops using an addictive drug, such as an opiate or opioid. Often, the drug user will begin taking the drug again to avoid withdrawal.

FURTHER READING

Hari, Johann. *Chasing the Scream: The First and Last Days of the War on Drugs*. New York: Bloomsbury, 2015.

Krosockzka, Jarrett. *Hey Kiddo*. New York: Scholastic Graphix, 2018.

McGinnis, Mindy. *Heroine*. New York: Katherine Tegen Books, 2019.

Macy, Beth. *Dopesick: Dealers, Doctors, and the Drug Company that Addicted America*. Boston: Little, Brown and Co., 2018.

Mennear, Sylvia Abolis. *Shattered Dreams and Broken Hearts: Fentanyl the Killer*. Seattle, WA: CreateSpace, 2018.

Quinones, Sam. *Dreamland: The True Tale of America's Opiate Epidemic*. New York: Bloomsbury Press, 2015.

Uhl, Xina M. *Who Is Using Opioids and Opiates?* Philadelphia: Mason Crest, 2018.

www.drugfreeworld.org
The website of the not-for-profit organization Foundation for a Drug-Free World provides information about opioids, as well as blogs, e-courses, and free fact booklets.

www.justthinktwice.gov
The Drug Enforcement Agency (DEA) provides "Just Think Twice" as a resource to teach teenagers the facts about drugs.

https://teens.drugabuse.gov
The website of the National Institute on Drug Abuse for Teens includes facts, videos, games, a blog, and in-depth information about drug abuse.

www.teenchallengeusa.com
The website for the international teen drug and alcohol addiction organization Teen Challenge includes information about the dangers of opioids.

www.drugabuse.gov
The mission of the National Institute of Drug Abuse is to educate the public on the causes and consequences of drug use and addiction, and to apply that knowledge to improve individual lives as well as public health.

www.dea.gov/druginfo/factsheets.shtml
The Drug Enforcement Administration (DEA) maintains fact sheets on opioids like fentanyl, oxycodone, heroin, and other drugs of concern.

www.cdc.gov/drugoverdose/prescribing/patients.html
The Centers for Disease Control maintains a webpage with helpful information about opioids, as well as the dangers associated with them.

www.samhsa.gov
A vast amount of research related to opioids and other substances can be performed on the Substance Abuse and Mental Health Services Administration website. The website also provides resources on national strategies and initiatives, state and local initiatives, and training and education.

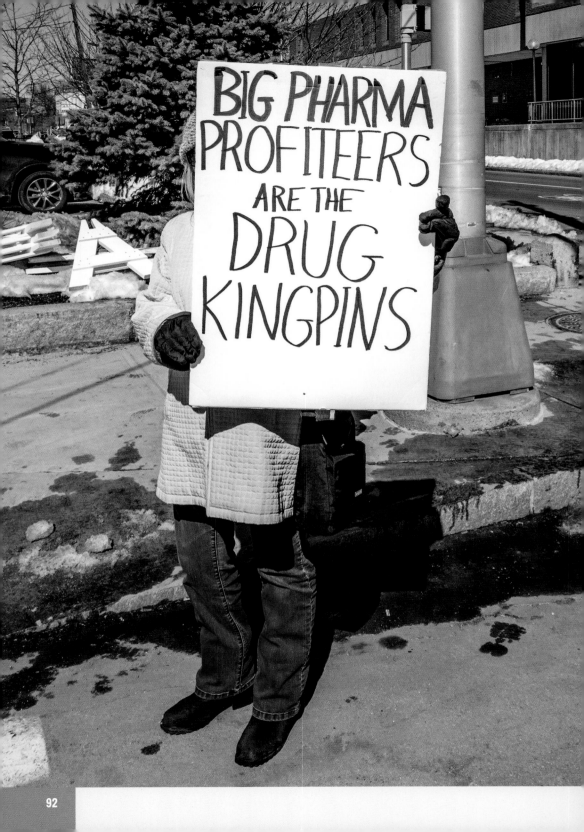

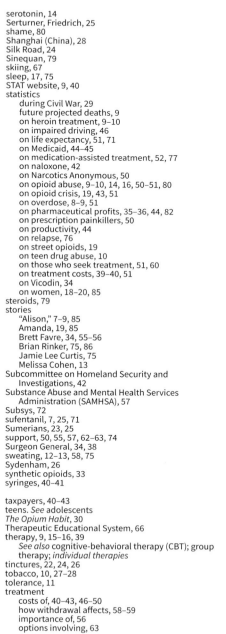

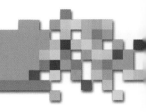

AUTHOR'S BIOGRAPHY

Amy Sterling Casil has an MFA from Chapman University and a bachelor's degree in Studio Art and Literature from Scripps College. She teaches at Saddleback College in Mission Viejo and Palomar College in San Marcos in Southern California and has published more than 26 books for school classrooms and libraries, as well as award-winning fiction.

CREDITS